Mrs. Tuck's Little Tune

Written by Cass Hollander
Illustrated by Kate Flanagan

Modern Curriculum Press
A Division of Simon & Schuster
299 Jefferson Road, P.O. Box 480
Parsippany, NJ 07054 - 0480

© 1996 Modern Curriculum Press. All Rights Reserved. Printed in the United States of America. This publication, or parts thereof, may not be reproduced in any form by photographic, electronic, mechanical, or any other method, for any use, including information storage and retrieval, without written permission from the publisher. This edition is published simultaneously in Canada by Prentice Hall Ginn Canada.

Design and production by Kirchoff/Wohlberg, Inc.

ISBN: 0-8136-0965-8 Modern Curriculum Press

2 3 4 5 6 7 8 9 10 SP 01 00 99 98 97 96

One morning, Mrs. Tuck was playing a little tune on her flute.

Mr. Duke walked by on his way to the bus stop.

He heard the little tune.

And before Mr. Duke got to the bus stop, he started to hum the little tune.

June was at the bus stop.

She heard Mr. Duke's little tune.

And when June got on the bus, she started to hum the little tune.

Mr. Ruiz was on the bus.

He heard June's little tune.

And when Mr. Ruiz got off the bus, he started to hum the little tune.

Outside, Mr. Ruiz's little tune got louder.

Luke was out for a run and heard it.

10

And when Luke finished his run, he started to hum the little tune.

Luke went to Ms. Rudd's market to buy a plum.

Ms. Rudd heard Luke's little tune.

And when Luke left with a huge plum, Ms. Rudd started to hum the little tune.

Mrs. Dunn heard Ms. Rudd's tune, and Mrs. Dunn started to hum, too.

Before long, everyone in town had started to hum the tune!

And Mrs. Tuck didn't even know what she started with her little flute tune.